Introduction

A line of rough-looking men waded into the river, holding rifles overhead. There were more than 170 of them—frontiersmen. They had volunteered to be soldiers, and this was their unlikely march to battle.

They followed a tall, red-haired man. Though they had walked for days, cold and wet all the time, still they followed him. At night, they slept on the ground and ate only what they could find along the way. Often, that was no more than a handful of food. Still, they followed him.

Spirits were low. And now they had to cross a swollen river in midwinter. In chest-deep water, their leader began to sing. The men joined in. What kept them going? The red-haired man would not give up. He was as cold and hungry as they were, but he encouraged them, inspired them, and made them laugh. If he could go on, they could, too. He was George Rogers Clark.

Chapter 1

A War for Independence

In 1775, 13 American colonies went to war against Great Britain. They wanted their independence, and they risked everything they had to get it. The colonies lay along the Atlantic coast of North America. George Washington and his ragged Continental Army battled a larger, better-equipped, better-trained British army.

To the west, there were British troops, too. Some years earlier, the British had defeated the French in the French and Indian War. That war was fought for control of land called the Northwest Territory. British colonists from Virginia had been settling there. This region ran north of the Ohio River from the Appalachian Mountains west to the Mississippi River.

Although the British controlled the Northwest Territory now, most of its inhabitants were American Indians. After the Revolutionary War began, Britain ordered the American colonists to stay out of the Northwest Territory. However, a number of the colonists set out to explore and settle the frontier anyway.

Some colonists established settlements in Kentucky. American Indians attacked the settlers in an effort to protect their land and hunting grounds. During the Revolutionary

Settlers on the Ohio River, Northwest Territory, late 1700s

War, the British gave the American Indians weapons. They encouraged the American Indians to attack the settlers. The American Indians trusted Britain and believed the colonists were settling on their land illegally.

As a result, these settlers were unable to plant or harvest their crops. Many were killed. They had to stop these attacks, or else there would be no settlements. They turned to a young man who lived among them. They asked him to lead their struggle to survive. That man was George Rogers Clark.

Chapter 2
George Rogers Clark

George Rogers Clark was born near Charlottesville, Virginia, in 1752. He was one of 10 children born to John and Ann Rogers Clark. His brother William went on to lead the Lewis and Clark Expedition exploring the Louisiana Territory.

A Virginia Boyhood

The family was close-knit and affectionate. As a boy, Clark had a typical rural Virginia upbringing. He learned how to hunt, trap, plant, ride, and wrestle. Relatives probably taught him to read and write at home. When Clark was about 18 years old, his grandfather taught him surveying, the use of measurement and calculations to determine the area, shape, and boundaries of a piece of land.

Clark had grown to over six feet tall, and he was strong. People were drawn to the handsome redhead. He was a man with energy, ideas, humor, and personality. He had an almost magical power that made others want to follow his lead. These qualities were not tested yet, but they soon would be.

A New Home in Kentucky

By 1772, Clark was eager for land and adventure. He journeyed west to the Kentucky Territory on a surveying trip. He found good land for himself, his family, and his friends. Clark loved the wilderness. Soon he returned, this time guiding settlers to Kentucky. He settled near Harrodsburg, Kentucky.

Clark became known for his skill in fighting American Indians. American Indians attacked the settlers frequently, fearing they would lose their land and hunting grounds to the settlers. The settlers needed help. Clark called a meeting. Men from all the forts in Kentucky came.

George Rogers Clark surveys new territory.

Virginia, the largest colony, claimed the Kentucky region. So the settlers decided to ask the Virginia governor for help. They turned to the young man who had shown them he could lead. The settlers elected Clark to go.

Help from Virginia

Clark told Governor Patrick Henry about the attacks and said that the British had something to do with them. At first, Virginia's leaders did not want to help. They had their hands full with the fighting in the East. Clark had to persuade them. He reminded them, "If a country is not worth protecting, it is not worth claiming."

Virginia's council gave Clark 500 pounds of gunpowder. They made Clark a lieutenant colonel (loo TEN ant KER nl). However, he was an officer without troops. He would have to enlist, or employ in the armed forces, soldiers from among the settlers.

Clark returned to find that the attacks had grown worse. Settlers were so fearful they could not tend their fields. Then they learned the truth. Henry Hamilton, the British lieutenant governor of Detroit, was behind the attacks.

Detroit, Michigan, late 1700s

“Hair Buyer Hamilton”

A log cabin set on fire during a night attack by the American Indians

Britain wanted to control all of the land in the Northwest Territory. The British hoped, with the help of American Indians, to get rid of the American settlers. In addition to their own reasons for fighting, Hamilton promised the American Indians supplies, rum, and gifts if they killed settlers. To prove they had killed the settlers, they had to bring back settlers’ scalps, or the skin covering a person’s head. Angry settlers began calling him “Hair Buyer Hamilton.”

Clark sped back to Virginia. This time, he and Governor Henry formed a secret plan of attack. Clark was to attack British forts in the Illinois country, near the settlements of Kaskaskia (kas KAS kee eh), Cahokia (kuh HOH kee eh), and Vincennes (vihn SEHNZ). Each settlement consisted of a fort and a town. Most of the inhabitants were French settlers, who did not support the British. How many British soldiers were there, the Americans did not know.

Chapter 3
A Kentucky Army

When Clark returned to Kentucky this time, he had authority to raise an army of 350 men. He wasn't disappointed that Virginia hadn't given him soldiers. He wanted frontiersmen. They knew how to fight on this land. They were sure shots. They knew what it took to survive in the wilderness. The American Indians in the region knew these men were worthy enemies. They called the frontiersmen "Big Knives" for the long, sharp hunting knives they carried.

However, Clark could not raise his army of 350. He managed to gather fewer than half that number. Even at that, he hadn't told them the secret plan. The men didn't know they would be going to fight the British in Illinois Territory. They thought they were to fight the Indians in Kentucky.

An American trapper and frontiersman

Flatboat on the Ohio River

Downriver to Corn Island

Clark and his small army went to Fort Pitt in Pennsylvania. There, they got supplies and flatboats. Flatboats were large, flat-bottomed boats commonly used to transport goods on rivers. More frontiersmen signed on to fight. Men and supplies were loaded on the flatboats. They floated down the Ohio River. When they reached the Falls of Ohio, they stopped. This is the location of present-day Louisville, Kentucky.

Here, they set up shelter on Corn Island. It was a good place to store supplies. It also gave them a place to train without being seen. Clark didn't want the British to know about his army at all.

American Indian wigwam, made of thatched prairie grass

A Plan Revealed

Now he was ready to tell his men their real purpose. He explained that the governor wanted them to take the forts at Kaskaskia, Cahokia, and Vincennes. Then he let them talk it over. They could go or stay. The choice was theirs.

The assignment was frightening. No Americans yet lived in the Illinois Territory. There would be no friendly settlements where they could seek shelter or get more supplies. French soldiers were still in the area. Nobody knew how many British soldiers were there. The land was filled with American Indians, who were fighting on the British side. Most of the men decided to stay with Clark.

Chapter 4

On to Illinois Country

On June 26, 1778, Clark and his army of about 170 men set off in their flatboats. They shot through the falls, where water churned around dangerous rocks. Just then, it grew dark in the middle of the day. There was an eclipse of the sun. The earth passed through the moon's shadow. It looked as though the sun had disappeared. The men gasped.

Clark said it was a good sign. This lifted their spirits. They rowed hard down the Ohio River until they reached the mouth of the Tennessee River. There was an abandoned fort there. It was a good place to hide their boats. They then set off on foot for Kaskaskia. It lay 120 miles to the northwest.

Clark's route to the Illinois Territory

Victory Without Bloodshed

Clark wanted the attack to remain a surprise. The men walked single file, as American Indians did. Their footprints would not give away how many men had passed this way. Each man carried his own rifle, food, and blanket. Along the way, they ran out of food. They ate what berries they could find. Clark's Big Knives were as tough as he had hoped.

On July 4, they reached Kaskaskia, which was under British rule. That night, they quietly entered the sleeping fort and town. Both were captured without a shot being fired.

Clark talked to the French who lived there. He told them their friendship would be welcome. He told them that France was helping the colonists in the war. If the French living in Kaskaskia promised not to help the British, Clark said, then the colonists would not harm the French. The French agreed immediately. Within days, the settlers of Cahokia also accepted Clark's terms without fighting back.

A member of the Kaskaskia people in traditional dress

What about the fort at Vincennes? No one seemed to know how many British soldiers might be there. A French priest named Father Gibault offered his assistance. He traveled to Vincennes and talked to the French people there. The French settlers accepted Clark's plan. Clark sent one of his captains and a few men to capture the fort. The British were forced to surrender the fort to the colonists. Once again, an American force took control without bloodshed.

The Red Belt and the White

Through August and September, Clark invited American Indians from all over the region. They met in Illinois to parley, or discuss their conflict. Their wigwams stretched as far as the eye could see. Many American Indian nations had sent representatives. Now Clark would need every bit of his powers of persuasion.

American Indian village in present-day Missouri, early 1800s

Clark spoke to the American Indians. He held up a red belt as a symbol of war and a white belt as a symbol of peace. He asked them to choose. He said the British hired American Indians to do their fighting. He promised the colonists would not ask the American Indians to fight for them. He also said that the colonists would beat the British—even though he could not be absolutely sure of that.

The tribal representatives discussed Clark's offer for peace. They decided on peace rather than war and smoked the peace pipe with Clark. Clark had used his understanding of American Indians to achieve peace. The American settlers would no longer have to worry about American Indian attacks in much of the Ohio River Valley region.

The American Indians accepted Clark's offer for peace.

Chapter 5

Fateful Decisions and Victory

Meanwhile, British Lieutenant Governor Hamilton in Detroit learned that the Americans had taken Kaskaskia, Cahokia, and Vincennes. Determined to take back the British forts, Hamilton set out for Vincennes. With a group of soldiers and American Indians who had remained loyal to the British, he traveled by boat on the Maumee and Wabash Rivers.

By December of 1778, Hamilton's forces reached Fort Sackville at Vincennes. Clark and most of his men had left. The few American defenders at the fort had to surrender.

Wintering at Vincennes

What move would Hamilton make now? He knew that Clark would return. But it was winter, and the rivers were flooded. Hamilton did not think Clark could travel in such miserable conditions. He decided to settle in at Vincennes and prepare for a spring attack. He sent most of the American Indians home.

Hamilton allowed a Spanish trader named Francis Vigo to leave the fort and return home. After returning home, Vigo set off to find Clark and report on Hamilton and his plans.

The Big Knives March!

Now it was Clark's turn to make a decision. If he waited until spring, Hamilton would attack him with a larger force. The Americans would not be able to hold the Illinois posts. He must attack Hamilton now. Clark wrote to Governor Henry. Failure, he said, would mean that this country and Kentucky were lost.

On February 6, 1779, Clark and his Big Knives set out for Vincennes from Kaskaskia. Of about 170 men, almost half were French volunteers. They had a 240-mile march ahead of them. Much of the land was swampy and flooded. Heavy rains were falling.

George Rogers Clark's men set out for Vincennes, March 1779.

Each day they slogged through snow, ice, and flooded prairie. Each night they slept on the ground. They ate what they could hunt. At first, they were able to find deer or buffalo, and they ate well. Then food became scarce.

Crossing the Little Wabash

At the end of a week, they still had 63 miles to go. They stood by the Little Wabash River. It was flooded so badly, they would have to wade five miles to cross it. Many of the men were already sick from the cold and wet weather. The Big Knives cut down trees and hollowed out dugouts for the sick. Then Clark lifted his rifle and stepped into the river. His exhausted men followed him.

Cold, hungry, and chest-deep in freezing water, Clark began to sing. They all began to sing. The big, redheaded man had rallied his troops. Everyone made it across.

For 17 miserable days, they marched. Most of those days, there was just a handful of corn to eat—or nothing. Clark lifted his soldiers' spirits. He joked; he inspired. His men took confidence from his confidence. On February 23, they made it to Vincennes.

Illusions and Surprise

Clark discovered that the British had no idea he was coming. He sent notes to the French in the town. He reminded the French that the colonists were their allies, or friends. He asked them to stay in their homes, and they did. The French would not fight for the British.

Clark ordered his men to take out and fly every American flag they had. The men were behind a slight rise in the ground and could not be seen. The enemy saw only the flags, not how few colonists were there. Then Clark ordered his men to fire on the British. Their aim was so good that the British had trouble dodging bullets to get to their cannons.

The French brought the colonists gunpowder and bread. Both were welcome.

Clark had his men make a lot of noise—singing, laughing, and shouting. He wanted Hamilton to think he had a large army. Clark sent a note to the fort demanding Hamilton's surrender. Hamilton refused.

The hidden Americans easily shot British soldiers who showed themselves. Hamilton could see he would get no help from the French or the local Indians. It didn't take Hamilton long to reconsider Clark's offer. First, he asked for a three-day truce, or cease-fire. Clark said no.

Later that day, Hamilton came out of the fort. He talked to Clark. He agreed to surrender the next morning. On February 25, the colonists took over Fort Sackville at Vincennes. They freed the prisoners. Hamilton was taken prisoner and sent to Williamsburg, Virginia.

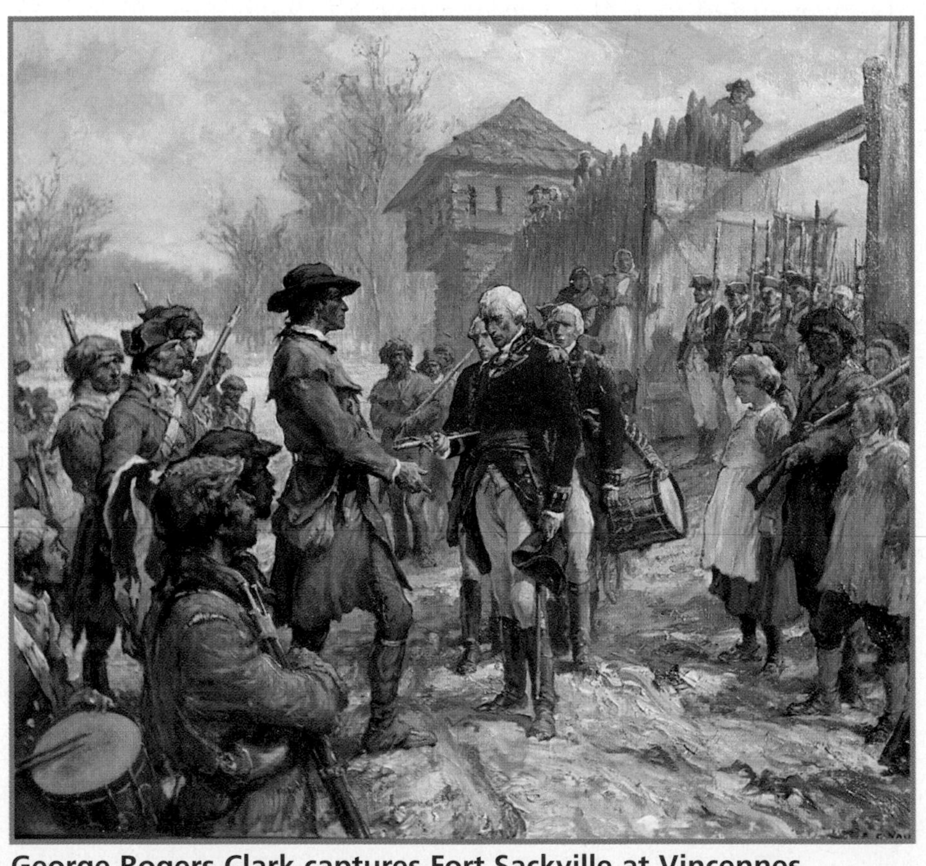

George Rogers Clark captures Fort Sackville at Vincennes.

The Americans shot a cannon 13 times—once for each state in the new country. Clark's mission had succeeded against all odds.

The British never regained control of these three forts. The young United States could now claim that land. When the war ended in 1783, a treaty gave all this land to the United States. The Great Lakes to the north and the Mississippi River to the west would be the new boundary.

The land won by Clark and the Big Knives later became the states of Illinois and Indiana. The rest of the Northwest Territory would become the states of Ohio, Michigan, and Wisconsin.

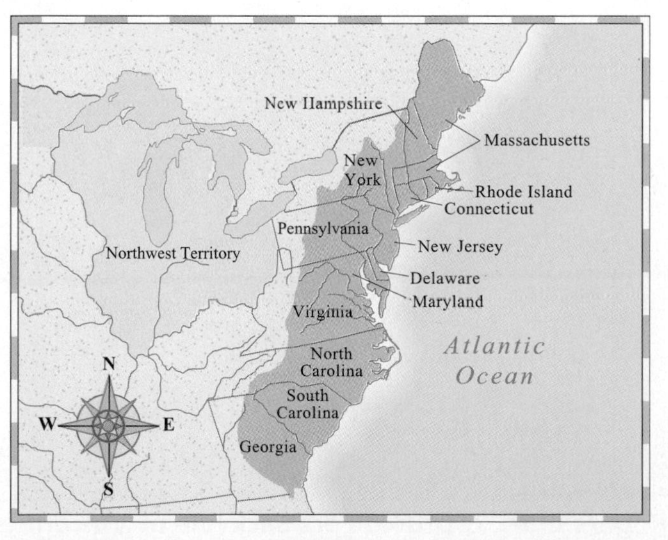

Northwest Territory was claimed for the United States in 1783.

Some Important Dates in the American Revolution

1775 • Fighting begins at Lexington and Concord.

1776 • Congress adopts the Declaration of Independence.

• British take New York City and win numerous battles.

• Washington's army wins the Battle of Trenton, New Jersey.

1777 • Victory at Saratoga marks a turning point in the war for the colonists.

• Washington's army winters at Valley Forge.

1778 • France signs treaty of alliance with America.

• George Rogers Clark wins at Kaskaskia.

1779 • Clark's army takes Fort Sackville at Vincennes.

• British invade the South.

1781 • British army surrenders at Yorktown.

1783 • Treaty of Paris ends the war.

Glossary

allies two or more groups joined because of similar interests

flatboat a large boat with a flat bottom

frontiersman person who lives on the frontier, next to, or in, the wilderness

independence freedom from the control of others

post a place where soldiers are stationed

representative a person chosen to act on behalf of others

rural relating to the country

settlement an area where a group of people have recently made their new homes

surveying determining the area, boundaries, and shape of a body of land by measurement and calculation

wigwam an American Indian dwelling having an arched framework overlaid with bark, hides, or mats

Contents

George Rogers Clark and the American Revolution in the Midwest

by Carmen McQuillen

HOUGHTON MIFFLIN BOSTON